# A Day of
# REST
# and
# GLADNESS

tate publishing
CHILDREN'S DIVISION

## K.M. Charles

Published by Tate Publishing & Enterprises, LLC
127 E. Trade Center Terrace | Mustang, Oklahoma 73064 USA
1.888.361.9473 | www.tatepublishing.com

Tate Publishing is committed to excellence in the publishing industry. The company reflects the philosophy established by the founders, based on Psalm 68:11,
*"The Lord gave the word and great was the company of those who published it."*

Book design copyright © 2014 by Tate Publishing, LLC. All rights reserved.
*Cover and interior design by  Cecille Kaye Gumadan*
*Illustrations by  JZ Sagario*

Published in the United States of America

ISBN: 978-1-63122-023-4
Juvenile Nonfiction / Religious / Christian / Holidays & Celebrations
14.02.04

Josiah's family has his favorite meal to celebrate Sabbath. This makes him very happy.

Ashley watches her favorite Bible movie. She feels very relaxed snuggled on the couch.

Lee goes to church with his family to worship God on the Sabbath. He is excited to see his friends.

Darrel and his mom do crafts together. He is very glad to spend the time with his mom.

Maria and her family go on a picnic to enjoy the beautiful day that God made. She lies under a maple tree and watches a squirrel.

Billy and his mother and brothers bring flowers to the people at the nursing home. This makes him feel good.

Raphael and his family play board games on Sabbath when it is raining. He is thankful that his family has fun together.

Katie and her dad go canoeing. They lazily float on the water, looking at all the birds on the river.

John's father reads him a book about the adventures of Christians in other countries. It's nice to rest by the fireplace on Sabbath afternoon.

Sandra and her family play charades inside when it is cold outside. She acts out her favorite stories or animals from the Bible while her parents guess.

Sarah and her sisters go on a scavenger hunt at a park, finding things that God created and collecting them in their baggies. They are glad that they can play outside.

Patrick goes to the beach. He tries to catch hermit crabs and minnows and find other things that God made.

Inga likes to fly her colorful kite on Sabbath. She watches it climb higher and higher in the blue sky.

Peter and his parents have a restful Sabbath afternoon. When it's cold outside, they have hot cocoa and bundle up in their favorite blankets and take a peaceful nap.

Carmela and her family visit other family members on Sabbath. This is the only day of the week that she gets to see her grandparents.

Yasmine's family and some friends go for a hike in the woods. She is delighted to learn about all the things in nature that God made.

God said to keep the Sabbath holy and that means to make it a special day. There are many things that we can do that can give us gladness and rest.

The Bible tells us in one of the Ten Commandments that there's a holy day every week and we need to remember to make it special.

*Remember the Sabbath day by keeping it holy. Six days you shall labor and do all your work, but the seventh day is a Sabbath to the LORD your God. On it you shall not do any work. For in six days the LORD made the heavens and the earth, the sea, and all that is in them, but he rested on the seventh day. Therefore the LORD blessed the Sabbath day and made it holy.*

Exodus 20: 8-11

There are many wonderful ways for it to be restful and fun.

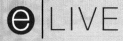

# e|LIVE

## listen|imagine|view|experience

### AUDIO BOOK DOWNLOAD INCLUDED WITH THIS BOOK!

In your hands you hold a complete digital entertainment package. In addition to the paper version, you receive a free download of the audio version of this book. Simply use the code listed below when visiting our website. Once downloaded to your computer, you can listen to the book through your computer's speakers, burn it to an audio CD or save the file to your portable music device (such as Apple's popular iPod) and listen on the go!

How to get your free audio book digital download:

1.  Visit www.tatepublishing.com and click on the e|LIVE logo on the home page.
2.  Enter the following coupon code:
    10a1-7c35-fe10-f831-096e-88aa-3b09-01b3
3.  Download the audio book from your e|LIVE digital locker and begin enjoying your new digital entertainment package today!